T0198845

CONVERSATION
WITH
A
SKELETON

Poems by Edward Fisher

ISBN: 978-1-4669-1182-6 (sc)
ISBN: 978-1-4669-1183-3 (e)

Trafford rev. 01/30/2012

www.trafford.com

North America & international
toll-free: 1 888 232 4444 (USA & Canada)
phone: 250 383 6864 ♦ fax: 812 355 4082

ACKNOWLEDGEMENTS

Grateful acknowledgement is due the editors and publishers of a number of publications in which the following poems first appeared:

Amherst Society American Poetry Annual: "Into the Keyhole"; *Atlantic Pacific Press:* "In My Comfort Zone," "Military Heritage," "Portions of My Animal," "Brainstorm"; *Avocet:* "Elegy for a Polar Bear"; *Blue Collar Review:* "Gargoyle"; *Caveat Lector:* "Bohemian Manifesto," "On the Care & Feeding of Poets"; *Black Spring Press:* "Cold War"; *Clark Street Review:* "Rummy's Metric"; *Concise Treasury of Alaska & New York Poets:* "Icarus"; *Fighting Chance:* "Sound-Bytes"; *HazMat Review:* "The Voice of America"; *Homestead Review & Poesia:* "Digest of a Soul"; *Hungur Magazine:* "The Moon-Tooth"; *Leading Edge:* "Einstein's Brain"; *Licking River Review:* "Conversation with a Skeleton"; *Mobius:* "Hieroglyph"; *Nassau Review:* "Plato Condemned Them"; *Old Red Kimono & Wisconsin Review:* "The Muse of Booze"; *Poetalk:* "Ode to a Typewriter," "Writer's Cramp"; *Poetic Hours:* "I Heard in the Midst of Noises"; *Presa 15:* "Uranium / Cranium"; *Quantum Leap:* "Realms of My Disquiet," "December* the Dying God"; *Sensations Magazine:* "Zapruder Still Life"; *Space & Time:* "The Eyes of Orion"; *Star*Line:* "The Estrangement of the Moon"; *The Journal:* "Death Kept Its Promise"; *The Leading Edge:* "These Creatures Are My Destiny"; *Tribeca Poetry Review:* "Madison Avenue Jingle," "Hack Hack Ala Kerouac," "The President Swats a Fly"; *Writers' Journal:* "Light from the Dead Adventure of the Past".

To my parents

"And death shall have no dominion . . ."

~ Dylan Thomas
(Romans 6:9)

CONTENTS

ON THE CARE & FEEDING OF POETS

BOHEMIAN MANIFESTO

Deep in my heart is an old familiar Bohemia
    Whose best poets died in a ditch;
No distinction is made there between love & art,
    The rhapsody of words or a curving silhouette . . .

An enchanted melancholy fills the air
    Intimate as the memory of a frosty dawn,
A Prague moon, a cathedral full of guttered candles
    And the faded domain of an outmoded muse . . .

In my inmost soul is a small café, a prison cell & a protest rally,
    A metaphysical discourse on fortune-cookies,
Nights of invention, a rambling passage from Rimbaud
    And a manuscript written without a single cliché . . .

At the back of my mind is a chilly village walk-up,
    A studio apartment with statues of nudes in dappled light,
A garret in Paris with a shared bathroom down the hall,
    An ivory tower & exotic rooftop loft full of pigeons.

I keep the key to my dreams locked up in a hand-carved box
    Disguised to look like a book of illuminations—
A dialogue with a ruined angel in the rain
    And the studied calligraphy of a spider-web scrawled in its margins.

Down in my bones is a lonely utopia, a pagan solstice,
    Traces of moonshine seaweed coral & a score by Debussy—
What do I care for your gizmos & routines?
    My lifeblood runs the gamut from freelance to frontier . . .

Expatriate of a shoestring serendipity,
    My threadbare vagabond shadow
Takes a cakewalk through your ideologies & taboos,
    Hitchhiking to the outskirts of a bottom-dog anarchy.

My scapegoat wrap-sheet is your banned, underground classic,
    The heyday of my sentences, your shock-treatment lobotomy;
My flea-market typewriter hammering out subterranean piano riffs
    Haunting as the song of the humpback whale.

Over my shoulder, in an empty rear-view mirror,
    Detours to a lost highway littered with miles of errant exile—
I dabble in the down-and-out, boycotting your protocols,
    Without regret, above reproach!

Instead of a bullet, a bit of rope, or a razorblade by the sink,
    I recycle your neon asylum through my skeleton hijinks;
My barefoot tantrum is your hobby, your truth-serum;
    Your crisis of self-doubt, my trademark impromptu kazoo!

I sit at a table by the window, waiting, despondent,
    Admiring a mundane still-life, an African mask,
Intent on a glass of absinthe, a whimsical gypsy enigma,
    And longing for an existential view of the sea . . .

ODE TO A TYPEWRITER

O typewriter, you are like some blown fuse in my muse-box
With half-moon hoof-beats printed on your shoes!
My metered imagination on the fly, electric-eyed,
Like some metallic Pegasus with iron-riveted wings!
Fusion of pen & sword in perpetual motion!
Trigger-happy Gatling-gun contraption on a shift-tab ribbon of steel!
Whistle-stop minstrel incantation of fingertip figures of speech!
Mechanical sequence of spring-loaded characters in bold-face folio
    gold!
My leafy greenhouse armory of love-letters in moveable type
Registered on a seismograph of sighs!
My jukebox efficient machinery of typographic whispers & shouts
Adding your rat-a-tat preliterate vision
To the laugh-track Laundromat rhythm
And tick-talk of my brain-drain

O typewriter, you are my log-rolling colloquial lumberjack Kerouac
Subconscious cylinder & sidestep-shuffle
Cliffhanger hairpin-turn & switchback bumpy ride,
Meandering toward downfall,
Keyed to my hard-scrabble Babel;
Fancy iambic footwork without justification,
Subterranean maze-work of gridlock & manhole
Vanishing up a fire-escape to a dove-coat
Jam-packed with jet-stream juxtapositions & random enjambment;
My by-pass into the boondocks, my exit-ramp to nowhere;
My ragtime boom-town nickelodeon virtuoso jazz piano
And legendary cane-twirling Little Tramp
Waddling off with a silent-era tip of the hat
Like a penguin on a melting ice-cap . . .

O typewriter, you are my scrambled alphabet of hysterical headlines
Hot off the wires of the heart, vowing *NOW IS THE TIME*
In the still-life hunt & pecking order of consecutive run-on sentences!
My rock-bottom cock-a-doodle *quick brown fox*
Scratching out the Chicken Little argument of the Cosmic Egg
Under the scarecrow ruins of the sky!
Your perfect circular basket &carriage returns forever
Over wind-blown cross-country pages in rainbow directions of rhyme!
Transmigration of souls in tongue-in-cheek secret code!
Insect antenna tapping out the night's annoying noises—
Lightning-bugs conducting an orchestra of crickets!
My dog-days hammering home,
Hind-legs digging up a starry bone!
Mosquitoes in love with my ears!

WRITER'S CRAMP

My motive was to nag the world with words.
My motto: bully the heart and its bloody ways,
Dare damnation, playing at the gadfly,
And rock denials from their glory-perch!
But on the white page where a poem should have been,
My cramped hand clenched the grim censor's pen.

A tantrum of language under my breath
Could not break through the lump in my throat;
Too shy to speak, too full of self-reproach,
My bogey, yahoo braggart—mister X—
Dragged his feet through each line, erasing my face,
Leaving a signature moon in its place.

Harsh task-master of my plans & whims,
Silenced by his own scribbled history,
Pinched image & shadow of self-pity;
My wretched symptoms, my insect resentments,
Pitting my bitten tongue against myself,
Retreated into their sanctum-shell . . .

This purgatorial circle of brooding
And cross-examination, dumbly drawn,
Gags on its own glibness, digging in—
This twisted nerve, this dead-locked iron mood
That runs along my shoulder to my wrist
And always knows who its next victim is.

THE MUSE OF BOOZE

When words there were not, booze supplied
Like some old hack the muse denied,
Some opiate that Coleridge tried
    That killed Jack Kerouac.

Those dizzy heights of vertigo,
Mysterious curse that murdered Poe;
Drowned in the river like Li Po
    By moons that hugged him back.

Bottoms-up heirs to Baudelaire!
Verlaine & Rimbaud's derriere!
Toast *ars poetica* in the air!
    My sea-sick drunken boat . . .

F. Scott Fitzgerald, Hemingway,
O'Neill, and Faulkner's protégés—
Rot-gut of macho's lyric lay,
    One skunk more for the road.

Speak-easy spirit, in your cups,
Hair of the bitch Absinthe's pups,
Hung-over, tipsy, hiccupped up—
    Kites littering the sky . . .

Like Dionysus' rhyme-possessed
Quest for the quenched bliss of the blessed,
Ambrosia flowing from the breast—
    Here's mud to dot your eye!

PLATO CONDEMNED THEM

Plato condemned them to the "Styx" of town
On the outskirts of the New Republic:
A kind of Third World of rhapsodic passions
Setting in motion a chain-reaction
That ends in a crescendo of light.

Pouring their musings into courtly ears,
They once enjoyed the sanction of the state;
Abandoned by patrons, left to pursue odd jobs,
Some became doctors, bankers, or teachers;
Soldiers, drunkards or crackpots.

Forced to stare, for long anonymous years,
Into the abyss of a blank white page,
Stringing together their own life-sentences,
Some perished by their own hand, literally
Dying to say what they meant!

Always in debt or depressed, out of place
In a world that would rather kill children
Than fund the arts, many, driven to madness,
Swallowed poisons, or drank themselves to death,
Succumbing to melancholy.

One hung himself by a lamp-post, another
Threw himself overboard into the gulf,
Drowning in a reflection of the moon;
While a few met tragic, mysterious fates,
Possible victims of murder.

One was shot point-blank in a lover's duel;
Another, running guns in the horn of Africa
Simply disappeared into twilight myths;
While many more were steered toward martyrdom
By the dogma of long-suffering.

Dante had the last laugh, damning Plato
To trod an endless round in limbo—
A somber pageant, unredeemed by daydreams,
Unimagined on the treadmill of the earth
By every civilized mouthpiece since!

ON THE CARE & FEEDING OF POETS

Bargain hunting for poets is a big mistake.
Pedigrees are not important but, if you go for bust,
A pedestal is a must.
Consult your local librarian, or simply visit a nearby café.
Look for one whose temperament suits your disposition—
Do you prefer the quiet writer of haiku, or visionary weaver of words?
The well-bred dilettante, or the atavistic wild man?
(The natural eye-catcher in any literary litter is, of course,
The rambunctious one . . .)

Poets love to chew the fat & relish a bone of contention,
Gnawing away at tradition & good sense like a comfortable old shoe.
A neophyte will rhyme all night
But his bark is usually worse than his bite.
Still, it's always wise to take precautions:
Keep a shelf well-dusted & dictionary close at hand
Until properly housebroken.

Most poets find sustenance from many sources
But generally speaking like their experiences raw!
Obscure arcana, classical texts, trance-states & dreams
All may figure into a well-balanced diet.
Many can be finicky, but most are prone to over-indulgence.
A number have sadly starved to death & suicide is quite common.

No elaborate grooming is usually required.
A sort of "natural" disheveled look is almost universally preferred.
Many males take readily to the unkempt Bohemian style—
Growing beards of varying lengths, dressing in clashing colors,
Sporting ascot or ear-ring, dark glasses & felt beret,
Chain-smoking Gauloise, or some such other affectation . . .

Though most imagine living in a cottage by the sea,
Many have been known to take up residence
In cloistered library niches & college workshops,
While a few feel only at home in a belfry or mental ward.
Others know no fear & must be kept on a chain!
One notable example rarely left her upstairs bedroom,
And several have slummed around the capitols of both old & new
    worlds.

Only a select few enjoy the security & peace of mind
That comes by being committed to memory
(Which, after all, is as close as one ever gets to immortality . . .)
But all are immanently portable, easily carried about for inspiration
And will fit quite comfortably in your back hip pocket.

AMHERST
(for Emily)

Poetry was her constant companion.
Her manifesto: a complaint.
Demur in her hermitage,
Compelled, in the end, to write, or die!

A pagan who could sing but never pray,
Her hymns & vision & prophetic hints
Probed the axis of truth—
Hours of argument condensed to a sentence . . .

Cosmic anxieties, flashes of passion hard as flint,
Written in the eccentric rhythms of a gossip
Let her fellow countrymen shiver,
Disrobing their self-righteous hypocrisies.

The rhapsody of a page from Shakespeare
Composed at the edge, sweeping like a fire
Through a small New England town
As its sleepers went to bed by candle-light . . .

The lady in white, by the cellar door,
Listening in shadows at the top of the stairs;
Her quota of quiet violence
A kind of insanity to be herself.

Homesick, hearing the wind in the orchard
Or along the paths lined with birches at night,
Everywhere else was a wilderness to her:
To travel meant simply to shut her eyes . . .

Her wingtip dipped in ink, untranslatable,
Demented as a housefly fumbling at a pane;
Her mood, Puritan as hand-drawn water,
As she turns her back on the world!

ALL WINTER LONG IT WAS POE

All winter long it was Poe, Poe, Poe—
Poet of loneliness, lord of the polar abyss.
    Earth had all blown into ether and ice,
    Wind mixed together with water and smoke,
    Murmuring mists with remembrance & woe;
Fires were all out in the empty empyrean.

All winter long it was Poe, Poe, Poe—
Melancholy messenger, laughing like a ghost,
    Orphan of the cursed & appalling snow;
    Nameless netherworld nemesis of man,
    Cruel & ruthless ruler of the damned
Haunting the night with anonymous obsessions.

All winter long it was Poe, Poe, Poe—
The doomsday engineer of misbegotten souls,
    Chronicler of dark crimes & the occult,
    The afterglow of corpses and decay;
    X-ray vision of history's shadow-play
Of endless, monstrous wars and grotesque inventions!

All winter long it was Poe, Poe, Poe—
Whose eerie phantom landscapes, in twilight splendor
    Reminiscent of the dream-state of matter,
    Preceding life on earth, recede in time,
    Mirror-silvering the back of the mind
Forever on the verge of a nightmare horizon.

All winter long it was Poe, Poe, Poe—
Convulsing in seizures—the psychopomp gone mad—
    Rekindling a crisis in the blood,
    An aura vaguely sensed, a throbbing vein
    That feeds a fevered lesion in the brain
Inducing elusive lunar hallucinations.

All winter long it was Poe, Poe, Poe—
That harsh, metallic voice, creaking like a hinge,
    Whose brooding mood, indifferent as the wind,
    Whispers over dead worlds and dying stars,
    Barking defiance, murdering the heart;
Silently showing the worm-hole way to extinction!

LAUGHARNE

His body was flown back in a box—
His friends stayed up all night waiting,
    Removing the nails to pay their last respects.
At the funeral, there was laughter & mayhem—
    A nightmare farce with mourners brawling
In the bars of the little seaside town.
    His wife tried to throw herself into the open grave . . .

Admirers of all ages filled the pages of the Visitor's Book
    And stood by the simple wooden cross,
Walking up the cockle-shell path to 'The Boat House'
    Where, sunrise & sunset, he scribbled & snored.
This "people's poet" who, during the war,
    Had caught their ear over the radio.
A cheery, cherub-like, companionable clown—
    A "bit of the boyo", bumming cigarettes, begging for money,
And downing the dregs of last night's party.
    A snotty-nosed troll, impersonating the "roarer"—
Great fun in a smoky pub, good for the tourist trade,
    With a wild look in his eye like a wounded animal
Caught in a trap, gnawing away at its own leg . . .

Becoming a legend, a celebrity abroad,
    He outgrew our thoughts into eternity—
Folk singers, rock-stars & even an American president
    Turned up in his honor at Westminster Abbey
When a plaque was installed there in his memory . . .

    Forever homesick for the leaky roofs of Swansea
And the dollhouse where his first child was born,
    Where his wife rolled cigarettes on her thighs
And fought with him like an alley cat;
    And his father lay dying at the Pelican,
His eyes eaten away by field-mice & vampire bats!

In the empty shed overlooking the estuary
    Haunted by herons & curlew cries,
The riverbed writes its epitaph to the sea—
    Scenes from his childhood lapping against the walls all night,
Receding like waves toward a vast expanse of dreams
    Where the wide-bottomed women with their sacks & rakes
Wade out in the sands and come back, harvesting the tide,
    And the deaf & dumb ferryman rows his boat . . .

On the spare table by the window where he worked—
    Vistas of golden sunlight with rain rolling in, gray as slate,
And a seashell on the sill.

#4 PATCHIN PLACE

A simple room at the back
14 x 20 on the 3rd floor
without cooking facilities;
only a wood-coal stove for heating water
    but
good light for a painting studio . . .

A quiet, quaint,
    tree-shaded court & cul-de-sac
with wrought-iron gates
off a narrow side-street in the Village—
charming alleyway of greenery
with fire-escapes to the roof and
ailanthus to heaven . . .
      Here,
the grumbling curmudgeon of Patchin Place
lived till the day he died; his beloved
downstairs in the kitchen, waiting:
an estuary of moments
away from the noisy traffic
and asphalt tributaries
    of midtown Manhattan . . .

In Japanese slippers & black muffler,
tea-kettle in hand,
the routine of his day began:
rising by noon, stoking the stove,
heating water for tea;
cleaning up & smoking his pipe . . .

Just enough time
to get down to the Battery for breakfast
before returning to his room to write,
    or paint, all afternoon,
recording the noise of the lower east side—
peddlers of smooth fruit & huddling nuts,
the colors & tortures of the "L's" roar—
    the words of his poems,
like expressionist canvases,
walking downstairs at *The Dial* . . .

Then, over to friends for a bath & gossip
& off to the nearest speakeasy for gin,
delivering himself of volumes till the wee-hours,
    spouting geysers of small-talk
after brandy & wine—
winner of the cocktail contest!
jailed for insulting the police!
indispensable on Edmund Wilson's
guest-list for the ideal party . . .

Allen Tate brought T.S. Eliot for a visit!
Pound came after 25 years in exile!
Dylan Thomas insisted on introductions!
and Hart Crane played the harp . . .

Marked for demolition,
harassed by landlords,
given to a sinking heart,
he kept a gun by his bed;
recalling those long days in prison—
one of the Lost Generation
wandering the streets of Paris
without any money after the war . . .

Alone with the moon
in the darkness of his room
listening to the City,
his little,
lower-case
i
like a candle
streaming in run-on sentences into the night—
comical learned ironic brilliant
grammar of boisterous revelry
        with or without punctuation—
imaginary horizons of innocence and love!
the downright damnably naughty
            unwritten pages of April
        intricately cadenced . . .

FIXER OF VERTIGO
(to Rimbaud)

After the poetry of the word,
An anthology of silence, of actions—
A phantom enterprise, an absurd
Adventure in renunciation;
A pilgrimage to remote places
Where nothing is named & the desert begins;
A blend of mirage & oasis
Where roads & ambitions all come to an end.

Laughter giving way to a sense of daring
In pursuit of "elsewhere", a desolate trek,
Disposing of unabridged dictionaries,
Hieroglyph graffiti & nomad texts.
His moods, like a deadpan moon: taciturn;
Mocking, ironic & cruel raconteur,
Waxing Promethean, in effigy, burned;
His own face erased, effaced in a mirror.

Fixer of vertigo, maker of verse,
He traded his soul for the sky & sea;
A voice for an invoice, a crown for a curse,
Becoming a multi-millionaire in fleas!
Accounts receivable, lists & sums,
Commodities for export, coffee & gum;
Haggling over silks & running guns
For Solomon's daughters & Sheba's sons.

Merchant in search of oblivion,
Drawn by ennui to the other side—
A negative film of illuminations,
The missing note from a gossip's suicide.
Posing for photos in turban & fez,
In the valley of kings, himself a sphinx,
With "nowhere" as his forwarding address,
His signature scrawled in invisible inks . . .

MISTER GINSBERG IN THE MEN'S ROOM

At a poetry event in upstate New York
Sponsored by a small town arts council
Admirers gathered in the basement of a local church
To hear Allen Ginsberg work a little squeeze-box & read.
When the break came, I hurried off to the Men's Room,
Followed by the Beatnik Bard, well-known to the FBI,
Who elbowed his way into the urinal next to mine—
Awkwardly unspeaking, avoiding each other's eyes.

Like racehorses at the starting gate, in adjoining stalls,
I recalled my favorite anecdote about Allen—
How he came to the podium in a state of undress
At a gathering of well-heeled dowagers in midtown Manhattan
Executing a series of symbolic yoga positions
Mistaken at the time for jumping-jacks!

I remembered, too, my sophomore year & the "Summer of Love"
When my old girl-friend & I caught sight of him smoking a joint;
And then in '68, at the height of the Vietnam war,
His picture appeared in the newspaper posing nude,
Hirsute & bearded, his left hand strategically placed
Like a fig-leaf, in some mystic Hindu gesture . . .
Prompting one patriotic American to fire off a letter to the editor
Swearing he *had never* & what's more, *would never*
Read even so much as *one line* of this infamous laureate of smut!

Having finished my business, I quickly washed up,
Eyeing him anxiously in the mirror—
His long shaggy mane, balding on top,
Gilded in the light like the proverbial "literary lion"—

While the imagined voice of my father
Drowned out all the clever things I might have said,
Warning me about how this long-hair, hippie-commie-homo,
This Dionystic wild man of words
Had lured impressionable, disaffected youth like myself
Down to his squalid lair on the lower east side
Like some kind of pinko Pied Piper,
Blowing their naïve minds
On his radical, irreverent flute.

In the years since his death, I have rehearsed in my head
What my self-imposed shyness would not let me say—
How I was the young Narcissus, fooled by the looking-glass,
And he was the last King of May!

HACK HACK ALA KEROUAC

If love were all that's wanting
Sold or shorn,
I'd kiss, at least, and be alive;
But I am harried,
Hurried through these lines,
Clutching this cup,
Attired in rags.

It's just that never stopping is a way
To light a new life up
And cough the old one back
(Hack hack ala Kerouac)
Tumbleweed bumming,
Slumming through the streets.

Yet never having known this I propose
(Apropos this toast)
Once the drama in your own veins
Subsides, and the champagne
Rises again: Be glad
At least, or plead for me,
For such is my condition and, my friend,
Such as I am you may be—
Undisciplined, abandoned,
Talking same.

I am part thief, part liar,
Part millionaire;
I am the mischievous child
Confused by a star, asleep
On the stairs, weeping;
I am the drowned boy in the headlines:
The little lost ones—
All the damned and missing persons—
Remember me!

This is the original image,
The enchanting fable
And the empty dream. Upon the pavements
Rain, the hollow sound
Of footsteps
Down the littered alleyways . . .

DIGEST OF A SOUL

I leave these words behind me as I move:
Shed snakeskin, dry shell of husked cocoon,
Chaff of my past life, scab of old selves,
Parings of fingernails, horn of the moon.

Over my shoulder, a broken twig,
Animal track at the back of the mind;
Scent of my manhood, envoy to a fig,
Haunting my body, half-life of this line.

Ghost in a photograph, forelock of hair,
Dog-eared mementos: my dream-house by night;
Molt of imago, the muse's foot, bare;
Marvelous larvae, leaf-mulch and mite.

Silence sloughs simile, sleep's folio,
A bookworm's bequest, digest of a soul.

THE VOICE OF AMERICA

INTO THE KEYHOLE

into the keyhole gores the key
open the door and let out the window

out of the mind comes the word
as thought lets out a mental shadow

the thought the word are the mind's composer
contriving conniving to bring it about

over the mind the sun arises
over the soul the moon discloses

seagulls riding green waves on the sea.
If ever there were time for you and me

it isn't now . . .

COLD WAR

The doors opened all at once:
Revolving doors in the First National Bank opened;
Small shop doors opened,
Curtains were raised—
Limbless manikins,
Headless torsos hung with jewelry—
Supermarket doors flung open,
Apartment doors and front-porch doors were opened;
All the doors were opened all at once
And the key to the city presented the honored guests.

Flags were hoisted,
Signs appeared
And the crosswalk lights left running;
In the center of town,
In the city square
Benches were cleared for the birds' return;
Newspapers, magazines
Left in the rack,
Smoke in the air
And clocks stopped dead on the minute;
Litter left in the streets for the proper effect.

The doors opened all at once
And the dead walked in,
Carrying flowers
Papier-mâché
Grinning mechanically
Chiming;
The doors opened and the dead walked in
Wide-eyed and perpendicular,
Pivoting at street corners
Smiling;

The doors opened but the streets were bare;
Flags snapped,
Crosswalk lights clicked;
The doors opened,
All the doors
And the old wars walked abroad.

ZAPRUDER STILL-LIFE

1

Concatenations of a body bereft
Of motives, moved through time
On a slab, its past determined
Forever by this moment:

Slow-motion of the limousine in black
Entering the mirror-world of the plaza,
Plate-glass & chrome-trim glinting;
Backseat littered with roses . . .

Crowds cheer at the corner as it turns,
Gesture and image vividly etched,
Bearing the dead weight of history
Laden with nightmare.

The play of shadows near a picket fence,
A puff of smoke, an open grate,
A little girl skipping in a bright red dress
Stops . . . startled by the backfire!

The intractable apogee of day
Collapsing in upon itself,
Sighing like a siren in the jet-stream
Out of earshot . . .

Dark regions on the surface of the sun
Revealed in a single blade of grass;
A ticking conspiracy
Looking back from a dewdrop.

Three hobos in a boxcar;
A man with an umbrella
Overcome by seizures at high noon
Seem more than the whimsical heart can bear!

2

Ratta-tat-tat of a typewriter's
Clattering keys, cutting it up—
Experience spliced in split-seconds,
Each frame blasted to bits!

Enlarged, examined, scanned,
Computer-enhanced for analysis,
Tagged and marked for exhibit—
Zapruder intruding in still-life.

The face-lifting of a nation televised live!
Sacrificed under the blinding eye
Of an unblinking god
By special bulletin.

All the great adventures
Of a once courageous youth
Sprung from that perfect forehead
Full-blown.

Fairness and breeding cropped out of season
Bloodied in the gore,
Witness to ritualized horror—
Washing our hands in the evidence . . .

In the subterranean chambers
Of the senselessly beating heart,
Secretly altered, inert,
Forever ineffable, transfixed

That head, that tragic head,
Too beautiful for November,
Lost in the voluptuous halo
Of a tortured cross-hair sight.

THE VOICE OF AMERICA

This is the Voice of America
broadcasting in special English
(English spoken more slowly
and using a simpler choice of words
for the benefit of listeners
who may have difficulty
receiving our signal . . .)

From Washington
here is the latest news . . .

Five centuries after Columbus
first landed on the shores of the New World,
untold millions of native inhabitants
north of the Rio Grande
are still unaccounted for . . .

In search of the Fountain of Youth
cities of gold were looted,
lush mountain kingdoms were plundered,
fairytale species & rainforest races
now number among *"the Disappeared"* . . .

Wars of extermination are old arts—
smallpox-infested blankets
and gifts of firewater
left a trail of tears to the reservation
for Nazi engineers years later . . .

Souls stolen from a village in the heart
on a dark continent,
auctioned off on the block by Whites;
cruelly enslaved but escaping their chains,
only to be lynched or shot on sight . . .

Over 40 thousand children die every day
on a global scale,
directly the result of secret wars,
on this worm-eaten Garden of Eden,
at the Big Apple's core . . .

Masterminds of media-mergers
dumb-down the defenseless young
hypnotized by cathode-rays,
eye-witness to senseless mayhem & murder
in the merry, merry month of May!

While the Greatest Nation on Earth
is building another by-pass,
another tower of plate-glass & steel;
leaving behind another sea-dump,
another moon-slick on the oil . . .

Planet at the brink, still shrinking,
nearing mass extinction, zero hour,
as the arctic ice-shelf melts;
black-hole in space, dark spot on the sun;
out of the nightmare barrel of a gun—

This is the Voice of America, signing off,
saying so long till next time . . .

COMING ATTRACTIONS

Ordained to dominate, subdue & pillage the planet, to over-run
    villages & clear-cut the land for sale, passing off smug excuses as
    self-evident truths; elevating greed into a Golden Rule, a God-given
    right written into the fine-print of fork-tongued treaties, blazing a
    trail through gunfire & glory . . .
The American Dream, like the Energizer Bunny, is on the move!
All those who resist are driven to utter despair, relinquishing
    everything, becoming the miserable mascots & scapegoats of a lost
    promised land.
Yes! Coming to a neighborhood near you, in wide-screen vista-vision
    & technicolor deluxe—a Vanity Production—21st Century Cinema
    presents the action-packed "Masters of Manifest Destiny"
Starring Uncle Sam & his band of Robber Barons—Daddy Warbucks
    & Scrooge McDuck—with cameo appearances by GI Joe & the
    Jolly Green Giant!
If you liked "The Trail of Tears" or "The Middle Passage" then you'll
    love the box-office blockbuster of "Structural Adjustment" &
    "Free-Fire Zones"!
If you cheered in your seats for Geronimo in "The Secrets of Skull &
    Bones", your eyes will roll back in laughter when you see "Mr.
    Potato-Head Gets a New Pair of Genes" & "Mr. Clean Gets
    Cloned"!
The very same people who brought you the extermination of the Red
    man, the cruel enslavement of the Black man & the heartless
    exploitation of the Yellow man, are taking their banner of raw-meat
    on the road!
Crazy invaders from beyond tomorrow whose bulldozer daydream
    pavements covered every square inch of the New World, whose
    mad ambition & fabulous avarice ravaged, plundered & strip-mined
    its legendary hills, polluting pristine riverbeds, denuding every grass-
    blade that stood in the way & leaving behind, in its wake, ghost-
    towns, mass-graves, piles of white trash & plutonium waste!
Enter, if you dare, the eerie nightmare history & necrophilia of war—
    the perverted creature comforts of a vampire class living off human
    flesh, experimenting with the secrets of life, engineering monster-
    robot blood-lines for the undead filthy rich!

An enemy-menace from which there is no escape, haunting &
possessing every human soul within the range of its cartoons, toy
guns, soft-drinks & hot-dogs!
Turning ordinary farmboys into psychopathic zombie killers . . .
The story of a nation on the rampage—swaggering, boastful, in holster
& bootstrap—spread-eagle Bigfoot colossus astride!
Half man, half horse, part ring-tailed roarer—who can out-spit, out-
drink, out-shoot & out-ride any innocent, unarmed woman or child
in sight!
Prepare yourself & be warned—whatever you do, don't come alone!
The sponsors of thrill-seeking scenes of primeval savagery &
uncontrollable defense-spending offer you this never before one-
time special free bonus bug-eyed bargain & goose-bump guarantee
—to shock & awe you out of your pants for the price of a one-way
ticket to No-Man's Land at no extra charge!
So hold onto your hopes & dreams for peace & freedom & the future
of life on earth, because the next incredible sound you hear is
America's big-mouth homespun atom-bombastic way of saying,
"Howdy, stranger!"

(Starts everywhere tomorrow—No one under 16 admitted without an
adult!)

GARGOYLE

Laughing the gruff gargoyle laugh of the anti-god of greed
Grotesquely grinding its giant millstone molars,
Decaying teeth and bleeding gums,
The tumbling Humpty-Dumpty doomsday bubble of Wall Street
Gobbles up another corporation here, a former nation there!
Swallowing skyline, horizon & sunset, gulping down ruined moons!
Its gutted ghetto grid-lock demolished cavity of a smile,
Glowing with cannibal Babel & heavy crude,
Crowing over the fabulous Faberge egg of a broken *nomenklatura!*
Dilapidated skyscraper jawbone and jagged edge of its mighty maw!
Lower eastside silhouette & sea-dump heaped with human skulls!
Natural habitat & last best hope of the heart going global,
Buried alive under concrete columns of gold-plaited actuarial tables
In X-rated executive office suites with green-tinted windows . . .

Arsenal of crazy democracy & the freedom to be dumb
Counting down to a homeless zip-code in the Styx!
Ballistic behemoth bristling with missiles & lists of missing persons!
Country-bumpkin government of, for, and by the peep-hole
Defending its micro-wave citadel of web-lust & alien-abduction,
Under whose monster-truck machinery and caterpillar tread
The hungry children of the world go unfed—
The empty O of their innocent mouths choked with ash and asbestos!
Pull down a pavement of stars over their starving, dream-stuffed heads!
Mainline their veins with toxic lead and propaganda!
The dead-weight of their mute, disposable lives
Transmuted into a luminous New Colossus—
Their eerie shadows seared into asphalt and glass—
Cumulonimbus mushroom vision proliferating over desert cactus!

All aboard for the New World Order!
Estimated time of arrival at zero hour, in Nowhere, USA—
A ticking time-bomb, a hole in the ozone,
A giant, gulf-size snake-oil slick & ink-stain on the globe!
Tickets, please; tickets—
Disneyland, Jonestown, Pine Ridge, and the Company Store nonstop!
And the bottom-line?
A million children murdered in my name
Bearing witness to the hollow cost—
While Rhodes and Krupp and Trump at play all vie to outdo Scrooge!
Merge their anonymous holdings in secret Swiss accounts!
Devouring whole continents for breakfast!
Blowing smokestacks over Babylon, belly-up in the smog!
Belching out bygone kingdoms and lost civilizations . . .

The simple people of the forgotten rainforest;
The gentle people by the fairytale river.

CITY GRAFFITI

City graffiti with seagulls & garbage
Spray-painted wall-mural, ivied with lives,
Slow-motion barges glide under a draw-bridge,
Whisper-jet airliners scraping the skies.

Concrete monotony, gray overhead,
Trawlers steam home with their fresh morning catch;
Up littered side-streets, the lights all turn red,
Ambulance screaming in siren dispatch . . .

Tugboats blow foghorns as ferries depart,
Substation power-lines, smokestacks & smog;
Mounted on horseback, a cop in the park,
Joggers & dowagers walking their dogs . . .

Cherubs in sky-wells, peer down from cold flats,
Flowerpots, clotheslines go by in a blur;
Pigeons on fire-escapes, stalked by stray cats;
Gridlock at crosswalks as cab-engines purr . . .

Grandeur abandoned, ailanthus at dusk,
Framing the stories of portrait-like windows;
Billboards & brick-piles where truck chassis rust,
Oz under padlock, dead-ended in ghettos . . .

Skyline & harbor are full of such moments,
Mad with the motions of profit & loss;
Neon mosaic, the hungry & homeless,
Greed-driven gods guarantee hidden costs . . .

News of the violence of history goes on:
Marketplace forces & free enterprise;
Hush of metropolis flophouse at dawn,
Muggers & cut-throats in blue suits & ties . . .

Bad dreams returning in one-way gigantic
Televised flashback of cascading glass,
Drifting off dumbly, out toward the Atlantic—
Heartbreak & trauma in chain-linked alas . . .

THE CHANGING OF THE GUARD

At the change of the guard at Arlington,
At the Tomb of the Unknowns, they turn,
Clicking their heels, ticking into position
With mechanical, clock-like precision;
Their eyes behind dark glasses, silver-mirrored,
Reflect an anonymous marble block
In freeze-frame, as the camera shutters click
And the ticking of insects fills the air.
Stepping out smartly, with a sharp "Left-Right!"
The sergeant-at-arms barks his commands,
Inspecting the bolt-action, barrel & sight
And fixed bayonet, with his white-gloved hands.
All spit and polish in patent-leather boots
He snaps to attention, pivots and salutes!

Endless plain stone markers in even rows
Pay tribute to the dead, whose deep repose
Overlooks the Potomac in early spring;
Its banks now in bud, or just burgeoning.
If you listen hard, you can almost hear
The delirious inner-workings of chance
And the hum of history's machine-like gears
Where greed and cruelty mesh tight in a dance
Which, if the innocent-young stand too close,
Will catch at their sleeves & turn them to ghosts—
Their faces, drained of emotion, mere masks;
Their movements, perfectly choreographed—
Toy soldiers, once lovers & poets, whose dreams
Are ground to stardust in that dark regime.

MILITARY HERITAGE

I belong to a military family
With a long & distinguished history
That goes all the way back to the Hundred Years War—
Armor-plate & visor, chain-mail, Cross & Sword.

I am the direct descendent of the Black Prince,
Of Agamemnon & Alexander;
Heir apparent to the stalemate & trench,
The horned & plaited tortoise shell, the stalking panther . . .

My tales of bravado from Babylon to Carthage
Trace back to rough-neck conqueror & Hun;
The Spartan shield, spear-tip & noble savage,
The Trojan Horse, the Golden Hordes of Khan.

My loyalty is pledged to cannonball & lance,
Lightning war, bayonet, magazine & gun;
When the Vikings burned down villages, I danced.
When the Vandals ransacked Rome, I beat the drum.

I was the staunch man-at-arms on the battlements
Fighting back barbarians swarming at the gate;
Over my fortress wall & barb-wire defense
Legion machines in siege-work sealed my fate.

Militiaman & mercenary soldier,
Commanding the ranks when catastrophe came,
I played my part in subtle maneuver,
Wars of attrition & dis-information campaigns.

I stood guard over watch-fires as empires rose & fell,
Marshaled my forces across the Rubicon,
Massing my shock-troops on the banks of Rhine & Nile
With phalanx & caisson, goose-step & robot-bomb.

My deeds with feathered quill once written down
Now printing press records, each bloody crime;
My lineage of violence, Armageddon-bound,
Older than Cain & Abel, fresh as today's headline.

RUMMY'S METRIC

Like any business, the business of war
Is shareholder profits. Win or lose,
Good returns are guaranteed on both sides.
Is it an enterprise undertaken
With an element of risk? You bet.
But the future is not for the timid,
And all other considerations fall
By the wayside when money's involved.
Do we worry a lot if people get hurt?
People are going to get hurt—that's a given.
Many millions, in fact, die every day.
Our focus has got to be the bottom line.
It's one of the costs of doing business;
Taking positions is not in our interest.

We have no opinion as to outcome
Especially in terms of cultures destroyed
Or lives lost, the effects on family & friends.
Our only concern is *total net gain:*
First, from the sale of illegal small arms;
Then write-offs for needed medical supplies;
Next, comes the haggling & back-channel deals,
Price-hikes on certain critical equipment,
All the no-bid contracts & privatization schemes
Which suck cash out of taxpayers' pockets!
In the aftermath, comes the rebuilding.
Will it seem inevitable in the end?
Of course—a daring history, a tragic play—
'Cuz in the long-run, we're all dead anyway.

Loose-ends? Hush-money & friendly fire?
Each covered up & plausibly denied
With double-talk, gobbledy-gook & bull—
Up the chain of command to the general staff,
Laundered through various departments,
Layers of bureaucratic loopholes
And labyrinths of lobbyist offices;
Not to mention the special bulletins,
The spectacle, the boost in the ratings . . .
Is war hell? You bet; it's a dirty business,
But, let's be frank: somebody's got to do it.
Women & children, boots on the ground—
They all have to pay! Nice guys finish last;
Playing by the rules gets you nowhere fast.

To decent folks, it makes no sense, I know,
But market basics still apply: fear & greed—
A game manufactured by insiders,
Not a criminal conspiracy, no!
Tho', we do work with gangsters from time to time,
Running guns or dealing drugs or breaking bones
To fund some undercover operation—
No place for sissies or too many scruples!
And all the camouflage & painted faces,
The useless orgy of mass executions
And indiscriminate murder is really
Only a distraction from the cold hard facts;
A mask, to conceal the collapsing star
Once our hand pulls out of the cookie jar.

MADISON AVENUE JINGLE

1

At the midnight anthem to mind-control
The hypnotic tickertape barcode scrolls
As spokesmen for free-market rigmarole
Collecting interest on an ozone hole
Drive-thru the window of your so-called soul
    In the endless struggle to make ends meet.

Our country-bumpkin son of Uncle Sam
Commander-in-chief & flim-flam man
Cooking the books in a back-room scam
Reality-program in TV-land
Shoots craps with your nest-egg & pension plan
    Flushed down a gold-plaited toilet seat . . .

Down in the Big Apple's worm-eaten core
Billionaires watch their portfolios soar,
Off-shore investors recruiting the poor
To join in the chorus for permanent war,
Genocide, child abuse, bloodlust & gore
    Where dogma-eats-dog on a dead-end street.

Lobbyist sponsors on mobile cell-phones
Making a killing, keep up with Dow Jones,
Building an empire of robots & clones
On round-the-clock mayhem & small children's bones,
Noses to grindstones in free-fire zones
    For Pentagon generals & corporate elites . . .
    For Pentagon generals & corporate elites.

2

Force-fed a diet of violence & sex,
Crisis & scandal & monster-truck wrecks,
Test-pattern images, special effects,
Lottery tickets, the latest high-tech,
Everyone's eyeballs were glued to their sets
        In the circus sideshow of our daily bread.

Narrow minds bury the news on Cloud-9
Frankenstein spin-masters stealing headlines,
Assembly-line tongue-twisters, sick nursery rhymes
Brain-wash believers deceived in prime-time,
Zombie accomplice to history's dark crimes
        In the Disney domain of the living dead.

In the master bedroom, on the TV screen,
Bounced off the jet-stream by satellite beam
Evangelists broadcast their pyramid scheme—
Lost souls converted & coupons redeemed
Outsource the down-sized American Dream
        And tuck it in a Procrustean bed.

Skyscraper newsprint colossal façade
Of cascading bad checks & lost credit cards,
Madison Avenue insider fraud;
Death-squads & night-shift security guards
Whistling passed graveyards & trusting in God—
        This jingle I just can't get out of my head!
        This jingle I just can't get out of my head!

THE PRESIDENT SWATS A FLY

The president paused
As the nations of the world
Watched him swat a fly . . .

An order to kill
Went around elbow and thumb
To a cross-hair sight.

His generals told him
The war must go on and on
And children will die . . .

So the drones were launched
And guided to their targets
With his signature . . .

The countdown began
And the heart was hollowed out
At its four corners.

IN MY COMFORT ZONE

In my comfort zone, up on Easy Street,
    I hear a key turn in my sleep,
My secret sentence sealed, without appeal;
      Controlled remotely from a star
      And monitored by hidden fears,
An eye looks down on how I think & feel.

In my comfort zone, from my ivory tower,
    God curls up with the dogs of war,
Invading armies storm in and withdraw;
      While dreamers snuggling in their beds
      In TV-land, watch talking heads
Inside their little box of shock & awe.

In my comfort zone, in my world apart,
    Depleted armor-plated hearts
Repeat false rumors & official lies;
      Proclaim the fall of Babylon
      Whose agony goes on and on
As weeping mothers watch their children die.

In my comfort zone, in my state of bliss,
    My agents work their graveyard shift,
Begin at minus ten and counting down;
      Behind the scenes, between the lines,
      Their engineers and masterminds
Turn hanging gardens into killing-grounds.

In my comfort zone, passed my fortress wall,
    My stockpile & my arsenal,
In desert shadows haunted by mirage;
      My real estate of unreal ghosts,
      All green-eyed, stationed at their posts
With phantom-limbs, glow in their camouflage.

In my comfort zone, darkly, through a glass,
    Half-men in bug-eyed ghastly masks
Redact a page of nightmare question-marks—
    Whole headlines written in the sand—
    While somewhere out in no-man's land
Embedded lovers whisper in the dark.

LIFE ON A SMALL PLANET

Nothing happens when you're happy—
One day follows another
Humming along like an old song
And you forget all the things you said or did.
Weeks pass into months this way, months into years . . .
Dawn pours into the room & spills across the floor
In slant shafts of light.
Dust settles on the books in the bookshelf.
The telephone rings all day
And the faucet in the bathroom drips all night . . .

Down the street, a lonely old man no longer walks his dog.
The people in his life keep getting smaller & smaller,
Waving goodbye in the distance—
A daughter's visit comes to an end,
A son leaves home;
And still, nothing happens.
The box turtle's shell is crushed on the asphalt pavement
Exposing its burden of eggs.
A bird flies into the open garage
Chased by a neighborhood cat . . .

On the far-side of the lake
The mountain slopes are stained with rainbows.
Two eagles tend their nest among the standing dead
As the woods fills up with the litter of leaves.
Everything waits & listens . . .
While halfway round the world,
On the TV screen, in the evening news,
An unknown mother weeps for her lifeless child,
As the earth begins to quake underfoot
And the tanks roll into town.

THE EIGHT BETRAYALS

In the lost garden
Where knowledge was forbidden
The ogre returns

In the nursery rhyme
At bedtime, the stepmother
Mocks happy endings

Brother & sister
Whisper secrets in the dark—
Promises broken

By the playground wall
Beaten, defeated, in tears
The friend turns away

Fluffing her pillow
Kissed & caressed & embraced
The lover deceives

In the smoke-filled room
Where the papers are shuffled
The businessman laughs

Down echoing halls
The government official
Misleads the people

In the chambered heart
Where the shadows grow longer
Each one is betrayed

THE LAND OF MISSING & EXPLOITED CHILDREN

"A favorite doll / knows the pain of a child's farewell . . ."
~ Gregory Corso

In the land of missing & exploited children
The sky is the same as it is in your world,
But everything else about the day is different—
In the doll-house, the battered rag-doll has a black eye;
In the sandbox, the toy soldiers have been buried alive
And the circus clown's buttonhole eyes are missing . . .
Cops & robbers play mumblety-peg, teasing the blade
Of a pocket-knife across the sad puppet's strings
As a jack-in-the-box pops up like a severed head!
The blunt instrument of the sun spins like a pinwheel
And goes down in all the crayon colors of a bruise
Over toppled building-block cities & broken homes.
The night plays blind-man's bluff & peek-a-boo
Under the giant cat's-eye marble of the moon . . .

Deep in the woods, across some barren patch of farmland
The children are playing hide-and-seek with their bones.
Along some desolate stretch of highway, the big rigs roll
Against the grain, in amber waves in the fallow heartland.
Sirens whine as matchbox cars collide & burst into flames
And the endless traffic drones on & on, night & day.
Lives lived in a hurry, driven, disposable,
Dumped in the snow along the shoulder of the road
Where a murder of crows pick through the litter & road-kill.
All the twisted souvenirs of tormented love—
The threadbare Teddy Bear with its stuffing kicked out;
The worn-out rocking-horse & discarded tennis shoe;
The mattress & box-springs where prayers were once said
In innocent witness before going to bed . . .

In the land of missing & exploited children
The little lost ones stare back from empty milk cartons,
On shopping bags, in tabloids, on the Post Office wall;
Their cheeks dimpled with surprised, unsuspecting smiles

Computer-aged to make them look like they might look now—
Pretty Peggy & Pat, little Jimmy & Jack
Who went off to play & never came back!
The amber-alerts & all-points bulletins go out
But the search-parties return empty handed.
The only clues—a bit of duct-tape & rope;
Fibers from a rain-soaked, torn piece of carpet;
A tire tread in the mud, a blood-stained glove—
All catalogued among some unidentified remains.
Still, the disappearance, mysterious, unexplained . . .

In the parallel world of the usual suspects
The alibis are all the same—a line-up of losers;
A rogues gallery of hang-dog killers with bad teeth—
Drifters, deadbeats, dirty old men & drop-outs;
Boogie men hiding under a bed in childhood,
Lurking in the dark corner by the basement stairs.
We look into the cracked mirror of their sunken eyes
And only see our own stupid grin looking back
Staring grimly through a day-old growth of beard.
Our fingerprints are everywhere in the careless mess
That escalated into some silly argument—
The impulse to anger, the drunken self-pity;
All the petty fears that set off the secret war
Waged around the kitchen table, behind closed doors . . .

At a bus-stop in the middle of nowhere, no one waits.
Keep Out signs greet visitors at the empty school—
Its windows boarded up, its Exit lights broken,
Its endless hallway walls, covered with graffiti,
Echo a hollow welcome. The classroom clock
Above the alphabet & blackboard has stopped;
On the chain-link fence, a padlock & a warning.
Only the forgotten sounds of laughter remain
On the rusty, abandoned playground swings in the rain.
They have all gone away, taking the future with them,
Their shadows fading, erasing their faces & hands
Like stick-figures penciled-in on a lost horizon,
Tracing the outline & shapes of rough-and-tumble clouds
Where grown-ups, too busy to notice, are not allowed . . .

SOUND-BYTES

Yesterday's nightmare is today's sound-byte!
We go through the motions of love, then can't.

What if the tip of what is, like a headline,
Like a glacier, recovered its tongue,
And the whole dumb, ineluctable hinge
Of everything that changed began to creak,
Calving an iceberg lump in your throat?
The history of the heart, taking shape,
Across a broken continent adrift—
Blowing a kiss to the moon, like a ghost,
Titanic—the Big Bang on your lips!
Repeated for the next news-cycle . . .

Today's sirens are tomorrow's flashbacks.
We go through the motions of love, then can't.

REALMS OF MY DISQUIET

REALMS OF MY DISQUIET

Moments ever rising
Silence is your sum:
Mum my muse of minus minutes
Fleeting on a falling planet;
Utterance of dumbstruck poets
Stammer at the brink, the poignant
Threshold of a gesture
Trapped by circumstance . . .

Shape of my estrangement
Faceless as a god:
Consciousness in clockwise motion
Inching toward a dream-horizon;
Body merging with prodigious
Movements of the moon to ruin,
Turning on its axis
As we turn away . . .

Mystery of becoming
Mingling with the dawn:
My adventure toward transcendent
Likeness of immortal voices
Stuttering in self-disclosure,
Outlined by a shadow's passage—
What might be my creature
Curving round the eye . . .

Realms of my disquiet
Haunted by a glance:
Song of solitude & longing,
Destiny & melancholy,
Solemn, cosmic mood all calling
Being in its natural prison,
Summoning unearthly
Murmurings of time.

HIEROGLYPH

Enthroned on gold cartouches
The jackal god entombed;
His lamps & oils & riches,
His relics & his ruins . . .

Around the central annex
On pomegranate shards,
A vase of polished onyx
Contains his bandaged heart . . .

Perched on his nape, a falcon;
Upon his brow, an asp;
Priests pry his jawbone open
With ornate studded adze . . .

The scepter of his office
Insignia & reign—
A token bow & chalice
In-laid with precious stones.

In awe, his vulture consort:
Midst canopies & fans,
Attended by dumb trumpets
With walking-stick in hand

While thieves, barefooted, plunder
His carved sarcophagus;
Scar ancient, cryptic letters
Inscribed on papyrus . . .

Into his secret chambers
Down winding corridors,
Unearthed, removed by scholars
His treasure-troves & stores.

The black-winged sacred scarab
Still rolls its ball of dung,
As Christian, Jew & Arab
Wage war against the sun.

URANIUM/CRANIUM

This morning
the conflagration:
mechanical dragons and pot-bellied stoves
newspaper print and graffiti;
kitchen matches struck on the rumps of priests,
metaphysical rhetoric over cigarettes and coffee . . .

Smog quagmire:
witches brew and sewage of the city,
ten gallon gallop through the gray
Grand Canyon loneliness of Grand Avenue
in the siren-streaked dawn!
junk jungle of nerve-ends and neon,
technological totem poles of talk-talk . . .

Bonfire verbiage:
tangled herbage of lung in the east
where the oblong moon
tumbled like an egg into anarchy;
dark-star cluster astronomy of entrails,
beast rising like sun in enormous belch and croak of Gog!

And the atom at the bottom of phenomena

split

My radio-active half-life mind
uranium / cranium
particles of thought
disintegrate to senility

cortical labyrinth
concrete reality
dread in utopia
isotope : hope.

THE ESTRANGEMENT OF THE MOON

Mastery of man over the stars
And over man, time's mystery;
Mechanically grinding clockwork
Of the mind's gigantic gears
Locking, interlocking:
Two human halves,
Two human hemispheres—
Cracked heart,
Split-brain,
Salt atom!

Interminable mountain of anger at
Your lips, nothing
Slivers of flesh
Parted for the sea's entry!
Slow-motion of the planet up a nerve-end to the eye
Opening out on giant spiral arms!
Whole continents adrift against the waves,
Each curved horizon merging,
Ticking, turning . . .
The serpent of the spine's divided solstice
Weightless, enslaved,
Like the moon on its chain of earthquake ranges
Rising pacific,
Bearing no name.

Further than the generations of the light
To bring you, out of nothing,
The unfathomable
Shape of O
Hollow, hungry
Baby in the belly with the sea-whorl in its hair,
Thumbprint of the gods upon the newborn heads!

THE MOON-TOOTH

Under its melancholy continent,
The old moon drifts through empty space—
A brooding empire of dry sea-beds,
Mountains in orbit curve into shadow,
Asterisms occult, at the back of the mind,
Governing my arm . . .

In a Pythagorean mirror,
The faces of the unborn appear, upside down,
Swollen with magic birthmarks;
Obscure arcana of Man-in-the-circle
Spread-eagle in the zodiac
Etched on my palms.

The heart of a Babylonian king
Killed off before the spring-tide ebbed
Mummified & embalmed in a jar;
The mathematics of silence eclipsed,
The mouth of the oracle entombed,
Ruling over a dead world . . .

After an interim of nights without dreams
The penumbra of an extinct god
Exhaling in vapors,
While the innocents are marched into the labyrinth
Where the monster awaits,
Its moon-tooth drenched with blood.

I HEARD IN THE MIDST OF NOISES

I heard in the midst of noises,
In the midst of children's cries,
How the heart is full of secrets,
And the head is full of lies;
And out of the sea of voices,
Out of the earth like an ear,
Thoughts underground, like a river;
Blood, like a migrating star.

I fear the bitter harvest,
My fellow man, my past,
Feel gods among my sorrows
And beasts upon my path;
The sun is dying in the sky,
The moon has come to dust,
And in the Milky Way the mind
Is dipped, the heart is lost.

A holocaust of children
Whose hunger goes unheard,
Martyred in the millions,
Murdered, massacred!
Like raindrops in the desert
Our tears do them no good;
The shadow of the planet
Longs through their latitude.

I know that in a flower lies
Some violence and some bliss,
That love's half-blind, half-naked eye,
Hides teeth behind each kiss,
And passions all go up in smoke,
Grief grafted leaf to vine:
O I have touched the snake that spoke
And bruised the grape to wine!

INSOMNIA

The night belongs to the ear—
The pulse of expectation & longing
Abandoned at the ragged edge of day . . .

Hour after hour, hemmed in by sweaty sheets,
Like curtains off-stage
The egomaniacal director demands another take—
Scenes of injustice & outrage
Played back & replayed in revenge
While some anonymous god pulls the strings . . .

The star of the show, in his cameo role,
Nurses the ulcer of loneliness,
Rehearsing his own importance like a curse . . .

Divided against themselves,
Body & soul keep losing ground,
Sentenced to cross-currents of feelings that collapse . . .

Unable to avoid the final judgment,
Limbo imposes indecision on waiting—
Sleeping without dreaming, dreaming without sleeping;
Waking without remembering if you were really dreaming or not!

At the end of a dark street longer than melancholy,
Near the corner of Saying & Shadow,
Someone is trying to tell you something—
Their lips are moving as they mouth the words,
But a car with a noisy muffler drowns them out
And the traffic light changes as it snores out of sound . . .

Down the road in the rain a dog is barking,
Gnawing at tomorrow like a bone—

A kind of hunger for nothingness
That turns out to be you,
Drops its disguise at the back of the throat,
Revealing the center of pretense.

THESE CREATURES ARE MY DESTINY

I am the Great Somnambulist
Whose daydream named the Sun;
My father was the Wizard-Beast,
My mother was the Moon.

My cradlesong along the Nile
An oracle fulfilled:
A womb defiled, a murdered child;
A father to be killed.

A crisis magnetized my brain:
Each syllable & myth
Inscribed like some Rosetta Stone
In Greek & hieroglyph.

The riddle that the sphinx was taught
In silence by the muse,
Divides my feelings from my thoughts
And breaks the old taboos.

The flint knife cut, the fire-stick burned,
I drank the blood of men;
Abandoned mother's milk & spurned
My history like a skin.

My heart reborn was split in half,
My totem animal
Took up the trident as my staff,
The hammer & the grail.

The bleeding lance, the broken sword,
Put out the hero's eye;
A voice, mistaken for a god,
A sea-whorl in a sigh.

These creatures are my destiny,
This cold decree, my poem;
Their love, my demon-enemy,
And this torn flesh my home.

PORTIONS OF MY ANIMAL

My body is a crucible
That I may burn alone,
This ribcage keeps its nightingale
In ruined Parthenons,
And rainbow-veined, my flesh outflies
Love's delicate nest of eggs!
O, like the firebird I arise;
My heart beats wings and breaks . . .

Earthbound now like a salted tear—
My afterbirth, my fossil star.

These portions of my animal
Are mortal, like the moon,
The parings of these fingernails
In tooth and hair resume,
And blood goes pacing to-and-fro
Down in its secret chambers;
A spiral shell, the sea in tow,
I comb the beach, a stranger.

The tick of time has sucked my blood;
The talking dead have changed my mood.

The convolutions of the mind
Uncoil to all their length;
Two climbing snakes entwine the spine
Up nerve-ends to a sphinx;
Enigma, riddle, noon eclipse
Primordial as the id,
Among the dunes and hieroglyphs
I built my pyramids.

My heart's a creature of the Nile
As timeless as the crocodile.

Myself dividing, cell by cell,
Out of the primal ooze,
Perfects its totem proto-self,
A hybrid, low-brow Zeus;
Evolving contours curve to shape
From embryo to ear,
My genius sang the sea to sleep
And dressed the moon with hair.

I cannot tell eternity;
My shadows come to follow me.

CONVERSATION WITH A SKELETON

I can feel him here, where my elbow bends,
Funny-bone working around to my thumb,
My brain-pan connection to old broken shin
Coursing down nerve-ends, pulsed to my palms,
Trying to get comfortable, under my skin . . .

"No bones about it!" he always begins
Rasping, with that macabre wit of his,
Contention caught in his throat: *"Your sins
Began with Adam's missing rib."* Worldly-wise,
Bookworm at heart, he loves to pick a bone.

My spooky, anonymous, gossamer guest,
Hiding in cobweb corners and shadowy thoughts,
Haunting the house of my body, like a ghost;
Whispering his grisly numbskull talk,
Gaunt scaffolding aghast at each aching joint . . .

Down-to-earth, wryly, on and on he drones,
Coughing up a fractured laugh from the pit
Of my stomach: *"Remember poor Yorick!"*
"Bone up on your Shakespeare, boy!" he intones
Sardonically whistling through an old cracked tooth.

Sick cynic that he is, he winks and grins,
Moaning & groaning, all his gold-teeth showing.
"Sticks and stones!" he insists. *"Oh, no, my friend!"*
*"When that sweet old chariot of yours swings low,
You'll forget, and leave me behind again . . ."*

*"Me!—Inventor of songs, like Orpheus,
Initiate of the night, curved in deep marrow,
Speaking in oracle-prelude to silence;
Prophetic, like a disembodied moon
In retrograde motion, out to the islands."*

"Bone of your bone! Your stardust nigredo
Your fossil connection to lost constellations
Mired in the orbiting mass-grave of earth;
Destined to be digested in the stars,
Eclipsed like an X-ray by mushroom-clouds!"

The argument of the unredeemed
Is always the same: sprouting through suture,
Flesh like a flower, vestige of wingspan,
Ankle and instep to tip of the tongue,
Calling us back to the dark side of God.

ORPHAN OF THE WIND

A trumpet sounds at the end of the world
And God, asleep on the anvil of the ear,
Grinds his teeth in his mountain deep coma . . .

Orphan of the wind, gun at the ready,
Man begins the song of Creation all over
Imagining himself equal to any task . . .

Plunging into fate, he decapitates day from night,
Shattering science & stamping out its embers;
Laughing out loud in the teeming marketplace . . .

Cavorting about in his fortress of incense & thunder,
His altar is a lion's mouth of monstrous vapors,
His destiny, a water-spout of black, dancing flies!

Calved in the labyrinth, in an ancient tongue,
Atoned on a scaffold of innocent blood,
His new god, Death, rises like a beast covered with scabs.

MY GRIEVING SPHINX

My writer's block is fluent in childish drivel;
His moods, like some unintelligible Babel—
A bitter, lost, untranslatable gibberish
With a lump in his throat bigger than Russia.

His mind is full of equations & geometric forms
Written out in Cyrillic & unreadably fine print,
Evanescent as the architecture of a snowflake
Or the twinkling mechanics of a stardust disaster,

His music is like a solstice piling up at my doorstep
Whose self-deceit is many feet deeper than despair,
Declaring his undying love to eternal winter nights
In terms more obscure than the Periodic Table.

At the center of his soul, the figure of a sacred lady
Is perfecting the mystical workings of history—
Elemental permutations & fleeting harmonies
In a word-game with Nature already evolving into God.

Weighed down by drunken orgies, the rhythm of his speech
(From his convoluted brain to the tip of his tongue)
Is the hardscrabble manifesto of the unwashed masses
Expressing their enthusiasm for revolution & caprice.

He is the epitome of estrangement with a big head—
His jubilant, grieving sphinx, covered with blood;
His demon-dolls & puppets & lyrical curses
Populate the melodies of all my gypsy songs!

With the sincerity of a suicide, he hammers out symbols,
Blending enchantments into nightmare prophesies;
The sighing of the sea is obedient to his winged eye,
Turning feelings into weapons with double meanings.

His heart is a miracle of flowering worlds & twisted truths
Binding the wind into moments of orphan wandering;
His lips are more red than the twilight drama of the Rose,
His joy more purple than a morning on the Cross!

BRAINSTORM

There is a storm that builds in me,
A dark sky dominates my brain;
A hair-whorl in the galaxy
Shaped like a hurricane.

Formed over light-years, cell by cell,
All thumbs in eerie elbow-rooms,
In embryo, a secret self
Revisiting the moon.

On time's hand-covered, anguished face
A ticking doom talks to the damned
And, sentenced to this blank white page,
Daydreams of who I am.

The planet falling, on the run,
Lost on some giant spiral arm
In giddy, clockwise motion 'round
A dark spot on the sun.

Apollo objects, cosmic clouds,
Stardust debris and meteor
Bombard the earth and blot black out
The reign of dinosaurs.

Rotating in a solar wind
Charged particles are ionized—
Ghost gamma-rays with phantom limbs—
A wormhole through the eye!

A haunting signal back from Mars
Transmits its static background noise
Where distant worlds and drifting stars
Are violently destroyed.

Gray matter of a world gone wrong,
Dark matter in the Milky Way—
Obsessions urge the night along,
Compulsions rule the day.

DECEMBER, THE DYING GOD

Somewhere between here and Sagittarius
Out there blinking, winking on the iris,
An inkling of the center, a winter storm;
And out of it, taking shape, a sea-whorl,
Some asterisk, this footnote to the night
(Always in the beginning without words)
Haunting the stellar stillness under heaven . . .

Ever at the unending, only ice,
Starting in December, at the solstice;
My shadow getting longer with the days,
My heart rekindled, native to the earth;
The dying god dragged indoors, its last breath,
Pine-dark and poignant, like a burning bush,
Spit with the sunrise from Methuselah!

VOCABULARY

After all the cheap talk about the soul
There's only brain-washing and mind-control;
On the inarticulate tips of tongues
The dram of a bad dream, like radium!

Under the hollow belly of the moon
The hungry timber wolf and arctic loon
Keep track of winter in the long ago
Vocabulary of the Eskimo.

Stark features of a prehistoric hour
Prefiguring disaster in the stars:
Whatever vision, trembling on the lips,
Accompanied an earthquake or eclipse.

Fossilized strata, lost worlds overlaid
With surface layers of silence and shade;
Deeper than words and the need-driven lie,
Buried alive in the wink of an eye!

Real miracles are never expressed;
True love is misunderstood at best,
Compelled in a language already dead,
Telling with sighs what can never be said.

Hoping to communicate the gods to you,
I mimic the dance of transcendence—a new
Utopia opening at my mouth—
Rivers of oracle, breathe in and out!

ELEGY FOR A POLAR BEAR

Trapping sunlight in his hollow hairs
The white bear wanders the frozen ocean alone
At the top of the world,
Cornered in his fortress of melting ice.

He has no name,
Answering only to the anarchy of the wind
In his den of snow;
His elusive shadow vanishing into a spotless sun . . .

Everywhere in those remote, lonely regions near the pole,
Like some half-conscious intuition
Fading into phantom thoughts,
He swallows a bellyful of blue fog . . .

Roaming the imagination like a ghost
Out to the edge of nothingness,
Playing hide-n-seek with the essence of absence,
He lingers awhile in the land of the dead.

A myth-in-the-making in an age without myths,
Noiselessly he prowls
In a place where no one goes;
A creature colorless as a cloud . . .

Come full-circle in that final solitude
Blending into empty immensity
The moon, like a monument to ruin,
Drifts silently through the void.

SPEAK THE UNSPEAKABLE

At the sheer horizon of events unfolding
riddle of man's unraveling
world at the brink
in a bowl
.
drop of ink
shrinking my shadow
sinking the sun in granite
inkling of the unthinkable abyss!

Through the grooved and confused maelstrom
and amazing maze of the mind
to the still center
like a gyro
O
odyssey, dynamo
beginning in the sea, in the body
and ending in this veined oblivion
this condensed mass.

Speak the unspeakable web of the world
weaving intrigues round my hand—
sticky, entangling, spun
like a spider's abdomen
x
-ray rated
radio-image of time's
tumbling Sahara adventure—
lips of the apocalyptic dancers!

Time escapes through a black-hole in space:
invisible companions drawing me down
vanishing planet, spiraling 'round
into a new
?
universe of verse
or wrinkle in the brain
taking the long way round infinity
to my thumb, in the wink of an eye!

THE EYES OF ORION

I am the giant Orion,
Son of the Lord of the Sea
And his stallions;
I wade through the deep.

The Father of Earthquakes
Brought me to light
Out of his vows to a dead wife
And the hide of an ox.

I am the sword of Orion;
Wooed in my youth,
I sailed to the islands
And rid all wild beasts from the earth!

Impatient in love
I did violence;
As I lay in a swoon, unable to move,
My eyes were put out . . .

I am the blinded hero
Journeying east to the sun;
Transfixt in the brow by an arrow,
In love with the dawn.

I am the belt of the hunter
Boasting my prowess,
Confronting the monster;
The virgin Artemis

Placed me in the night sky
With scorpions at my feet.
Remarkable to the naked eye
I seek the sweet, sister stars!

I am the light of Orion,
Wearing the hide of the lion;
Slayer of nightmares,
Ghost of the light-years.

LIGHT FROM THE DEAD ADVENTURE
OF THE PAST

Light from the dead adventure of the past—
Disaster in a spectacle of dust,
A spectral sight a billion light-years off—
Bombards the eye with photons, stellar stuff;
Debris of lost worlds whisper what we are:
Deposits of evolving cosmos come
With galaxies at fingertip and thumb
To take up pure invention in the stars!

Beyond the huge penumbra of a dream,
Emerging from a nerve-end in the night
That curves along a blind-spot to the brain;
Across an arctic cataract, blank, white,
    The dark-side of the moon moves on the mind
    Meeting this page, leaving this poem behind.

EINSTEIN'S BRAIN

What's left of Einstein's brain is kept in a jar at the unemployment
    office.
The keys to his eyes are in a safety deposit box at the First National
    Bank.
His ashes, scattered like a handful of stars, are laughing in dark matter.
Immortality to him was a fantasy, a fable, and the Bible, a bedtime
    story.
Only mathematics could rival the Psalms & the teachings of Buddha.

When time was discovered at the Swiss Patent Office
All the clocks in town stopped & watchmakers looked up from their
    work.
Passengers on tram-cars riding a beam of light never arrived.
Observers setting off at the same time ended up in another universe.
Every question-mark became a black-hole, every thought a parallel
    world.

Alone in his room, with pencil & pad, he turned the sky upside down
Scribbling the structure of galaxies on the back of a folded envelop.
What we call idle daydreams, he called "thought experiments"
Keeping a year of miracles in a file-drawer at the Department of
    Physics
Where every paper-clip on his desk contained an apocalypse.

A man without a country, he left no forwarding address behind.
He liked to pretend he was only visiting earth from another planet.
His biggest mistake in life was signing his name on a letter to the
    president.
After that, the voice of authority started talking over everyone's head
And even idlers at sidewalk cafes came under suspicion by the FBI.

He got his best ideas from reading the works of Dostoyevsky
And found happiness by making friends with a few small animals.
He was the lady's man at the cocktail party who played the violin—
The one at the Zurich railway station holding a bouquet of red flowers;
The clown sticking his tongue out at the bottom of Pandora's box.

In the years that followed, the unfathomably bizarre became
    commonplace.
Every insect & star seemed to dance to the same mysterious tune
And the fate of the human race hinged on the wings of the honeybee.
God's power was found in every atom, but nowhere in the hearts of
    men,
Proving the improbability of any paradise based on a roll of the dice.

The future he imagined at 21 turned out to be a pacifist's worst
    nightmare;
He gambled his family & married life away for a little Nobel Prize
    money
And conducted lecturers at Cambridge wearing carpet slippers without
    socks.
He loved sailing & kept up a salty correspondence with Marilyn
    Monroe,
Reducing everything to the formula "Boredom Equals Eternity".

I saw him last night splitting hairs in the halo-nimbus of a solar eclipse,
His lonely ghost winking back at me from a singing singularity.
Imagination curved around his elbow toward a thumbprint in cosmic
    awe;
The moon played hide-n-seek with time & space out in the Milky Way
Where the simple wonder in a child's eyes is our only compass rose!

About the Author

Edward Fisher was born in Ohio & spent his boyhood as a military brat, touring castles on the Rhine & strolling down the Champs Elysees. As a teenager in the 60s, he watched tanks roll through the Heart of Dixie on their way to Ole Miss & rode out an earthquake in Alaska. After graduating with a bachelors in Literature from Reed College in Portland, Oregon, he joined the Peace Corps, surviving his tour of service in Uganda in the aftermath of Idi Amin's bloody coup. He holds a doctorate in psychology & worked with special needs children as a play therapist & adventure-based counselor. He is currently living with his wife and two children in the foothills of the Catskills in upstate New York. This is his first book of poems.